I0103681

Common Sense for a Dying Nation
Copyright © 2023 Jonah Schulz

ISBN 978-1-948613-20-0

Library of Congress Control Number: 2023900603

Printed in the United States of America

Sunny Day Publishing, LLC
Cuyahoga Falls, Ohio 44223
www.sunnydaypublishing.com
editor@sunnydaypublishing.com

For My Mother

*Who showed me that
there is no greater endeavor
than seeking truth, beauty,
and love.*

Common Sense
For A Dying Nation

*** * ***

Jonah Schulz

Introduction

This small book is written with a singular purpose. It is not to advance the agenda of any person, party, or corporation, but rather to inspire the reader to critically think about the past, present, and future states of our rights and government.

Very few people in our United States believe that we are headed in the proper direction. In fact, this is one of the few topics we can agree upon. It is hard to say if we have ever lived in a time as divided and incoherent as we are now. The world has changed so rapidly and drastically that the small ponds that once represented our philosophical differences have grown into oceans that seemingly no bridge can cover.

It is apparent that much of this change has been generally positive, yet equally as much has been a detriment to society. Nearly all of us have grown up and lived in a time of peace and prosperity that has never before been seen on this earth. Most have lived life with relative ease compared to the brutal crawl of history when men warred, toiled, and endured harsh injustices that we have been sheltered from within our borders. The life of the average American has turned almost exclusively to commerce and materialism. This has made us exceedingly comfortable by historical standards, but has taken our eyes off the foundational elements of what creates a free society and a happy life. This negligence has opened the doors to charlatans and ne'er-do-wells who seek to infiltrate our lives and achieve ultimate authority over the individual.

As Thomas Jefferson said at the founding of our Republic, "The price of freedom is eternal vigilance," and our blinders have been on for quite some time. Since we have lost sight and direction as a nation, we must work from the ground up, rediscover ourselves, and reawaken the basic understanding of what America ought to be. The following text will hopefully serve as a guide – A guide to diagnose our problems and prescribe fundamental solutions that advance the liberty and prosperity of every American.

"In the following pages I offer nothing more than simple facts, plain arguments, and common sense: and have no other preliminaries to settle with the reader, than that he will divest himself of prejudice and prepossession, and suffer his reason and his feelings to determine for themselves: that he will put on, or rather that he will not put off, the true character of a man, and generously enlarge his views beyond the present day."

— Thomas Paine, "Common Sense," 1776

The Natural Rights of Man

We cannot have a coherent conversation on the United States of America without first agreeing on what is foundational and inherent. Our nation was founded on the very basic truth that man has natural rights. Rights that cannot be separated from man — meaning that at all times, regardless of law, government, or leadership, these rights remain with the individual. And further, that these rights are either being naturally fulfilled or unnaturally infringed upon — meaning they cannot ever be taken or given by an individual or government. Without first agreeing upon this universal truth, we cannot hope to come together on any of the specific issues and disagreements we face.

But to agree even on this truth, we must also agree on two others. First, we must agree, regardless of religious or philosophical background, that human beings are more than empty vessels, more than mindless animals, more than sacks of blood and bone. We must agree that human beings, as individuals and as a collective, have essential and unique purpose and responsibilities. We must agree that human beings were not created or placed on this earth to simply float through an empty life, die, and be buried

In summation, we must agree that we are indeed created with a greater purpose than simply existing. Because if we merely exist, if we are not made to serve something greater, if we are nothing more than animals lucky enough to have achieved a higher intellect, then we are simply at the mercy of the attitudes of the time and place in which we live. No rights can be inherent to a people who consider themselves nothing more than cattle.

Second, we must agree that there is a true and just moral center — that what is right and wrong does not change based on time, place and attitude of the individual, or person. I do not submit that there is no gray area, or that there is no room for debate on what should be considered right, just, and acceptable. Much of what is truly right and wrong we may not know with certainty until we are with our Creator. What I do submit is that there is one truth. That although we may not have the answer, right and wrong are always existing and never changing.

Much of the debate in America today comes down to this very subject. We now live in an age of "my truth," or a simple belief that there is no universal truth or rule of order but rather that truth and reality itself is subject to the will and caprices of the individual. Though many use the term "my truth" innocently, as a stand-in for their personal perspective or life experiences, it is also used to squash any argument that goes against one's personal belief or perception of the world.

This worldview cannot long last in a free society. For example, it was Hitler's "personal truth" that drove him to murder six million Jews. It was George Wallace's "personal truth" that led him to fight for segregation. And it is the personal truth of many billions of people throughout world history that has led them to believe, say, and do things not only harmful to individuals and society, but offensive to our very nature as human beings.

If our idea of truth and justice is simply dependent on either our own personal outlook or the opinion of the majority, then many of history's most brutal acts cannot be deemed wrong or unnatural. How can we label brutality, murder, and injustice as wrong with such certainty? If there is no moral center or universal truth, then these atrocities may be hard to stomach, but they cannot be labeled right or wrong. And if rights, truth, and justice are not firmly held to an unwavering moral center, man has no universal or natural rights — he has only temporary privileges granted to him by whatever current power lords over him.

However, if we can agree that there is such a thing as an unchanging, true moral center, then we must agree that man does indeed have inherent rights yesterday, today, and always. That these rights cannot be taken or given but are natural and just.

These basic beliefs are the staple of American society and culture — and what has made our nation different from any other civilization in world history. Before our nation's founding, never before had man made such a claim — that his rights were not of this earth, but rather, divine. As a country, we once had nearly universal agreement on this premise, but much of our understanding has faded over the decades of security and commerce that have become the primary focus of our lives. In order to move forward, we must first embrace our foundation that man can neither add nor subtract from our inherent rights.

We speak much of liberty, freedom, and rights in America, but do we really know what these words mean beyond vague patriotic slogans? Do we remember what belongs to us? In order to have an intelligent debate on policy or government, we must first discuss what these natural rights look like in their purest form.

In a utopian society in which men are not at the mercy of temptation and sin, where what is good and natural reigns supreme in our hearts, there would be no need for government or law. Men would naturally live out their inherent rights without any impediments. We would be safe and secure without any fear of physical harm, theft, or control over our bodily decisions. We would speak openly and freely without any fear of violence, persecution, or censorship. We would have total control over our property, materials, and businesses without fear of outside intervention.

Although in this perfect world we would have little to fear, we would have the ability to defend our loved ones, our property, and ourselves from harm. We would have the sovereignty to purely and justly select leaders and structures for our society that empower the individual and the collective. Our commerce would be unimpeded by external forces. Our families would fall solely under the jurisdiction of the household without dictates from other powers. We would engage in spiritual and religious practices that fulfill our human nature without interference. And most importantly, we would be free to dictate our own lives and destinies. All of these rights would be allowed to every individual without exception.

This is a vision of the world if man lived in harmony with his intended purpose. With these most basic rights, every individual on this earth would have the purest opportunity to live a happy, healthy, and prosperous life. Envision this world totally uninhibited by violence, greed, lust, and ill will. This is freedom and liberty unadulterated.

But we do not live in this utopia and none of us will ever be free from temptation and vice. So how do these rights — this liberty — exist in a world filled with flawed men? For this reason, governments are instituted among men. As best put by James Madison: "If men were angels, no government would be necessary."

The sole and pure purpose of government is

to defend the liberty of the individual and family. For example, an individual has the right to life and his own property. Due to the nature of man, an individual will face threats to this life and property in many ways. Men with wicked intentions will attempt to damage and take life and property. For this reason, a government is formed with laws and enforcement mechanisms that deter such actions, suppress man's worst impulses, and deliver justice when necessary. Because humans will naturally create hierarchies and societal structures out of necessity for safety and security of our rights, a government of some form will always exist in a free society.

The debate then turns to what form of government is best suited to create this free society. Some will argue for a government that hardly exists. That a tiny government will allow individuals maximum power and authority over their own lives. Others will advocate for a government that serves, in many ways, as a caretaker providing goods and services to its people. That a larger, more involved government will create security and allow individuals to pursue other freedoms less burdened by basic needs.

The best government is that which maximizes both liberty and virtue. In modern society, we have forgotten what liberty truly is. Liberty is not simply getting what you want, doing what you feel and pursuing your most base desires. Our Founding Fathers understood this. Liberty is being free to pursue what is good, true and beautiful. The goal of liberty is not money, it is not physical gratification or a life without rules — happiness and fulfillment are the ultimate goals of liberty. To understand this, we must ponder what it means to be truly free.

Some may argue for total and absolute bodily autonomy in the form of unimpeded drug use. Should society perceive the heroin addict as a free man if there are no laws to curb or condemn his behavior? Or should society rightfully perceive the truth – that there is no liberty, that he is not free, that he is a slave to his most base desires. We must perceive that men pursuing these desires will never find the path to happiness and fulfillment. As a result, we sacrifice what some may perceive as certain freedoms to allow for an overall betterment of society and ourselves. We must discern liberty from licentiousness. Only then will our natural rights be affirmed.

Some may view this as a balancing act — and

they would be right. Living in a free society often goes against the tendencies and default setting of mankind and therefore requires constant oversight and recalibration. Rights and truth are eternal, but our world is ever-changing. For this reason, we once understood the necessity of self-government — that while law and government exist to regulate people, we exist to regulate the government and law.

The default state of humanity is hunger, war and slavery. Beginning in 1776, that finally began to change. For all of human history, a select few monarchs and oligarchs ruled over society, viewed common men as pawns and human rights as expendable to their ends. So, what ultimately changed? Was it simply a form of government instituted to defend the people? Was it as simple as putting a pen to paper and creating a few new laws? Or is freedom preserved more in the hearts of men than in the halls of government?

I would submit to you that the average person in America is less free today than at the time we were born. We have more material comforts — that is beyond dispute — but we have sacrificed every ounce of our true liberty for a softer, more docile existence. Our government, corporations, and wealthy oligarchs now wield power that is beyond comprehension and the average American has virtually no power over the decisions being made over his own life. Did this happen because our form of government is flawed or because we have forgotten what it means to be free?

I would argue that the flame of freedom has been extinguished in our hearts and if we wish to restore and preserve the rights we once cherished, there must be a reawakening of liberty in our very souls. The Founders of America argued that a life without natural rights is not a life worth living. I would make the same claim today.

What Makes a Nation?

In order to grapple with the issues plaguing the United States, we must first envision what a unified nation looks like. We have been conditioned to believe that a nation is simply made as arbitrary lines are drawn and redrawn through colonization and conquest. While it is true that this is how many nations have found their origins, it is not how one is maintained. Strength and force can form only temporary bonds as true unity and longevity come through agreements and understanding among the people.

One can take a brief look around America to see that the bonds that once held strong are fraying if not coming undone altogether. As we have seen throughout history, any nation that is at war with itself will not long stand. The nature of the world is such that external forces will always attempt to encroach on the borders, resources and sovereignty of nations. But more often than not, the demise of a nation begins with an internal decay. So, what cornerstones must be maintained to stave off collapse?

First, there must be a shared culture. This does not mean there isn't room for variety and difference throughout a nation. Every country throughout history has had regions with their own specialties and interests. We should never expect Kansas and California to have no distinction. However, mutual beliefs must be held throughout a nation to form the glue holding millions of people together in relative peace. This becomes increasingly difficult in a nation like America, as we are formed out of many people and many cultures. Nearly every nation on the globe is represented in one way, shape or form within our borders, and these cultural differences have become ever more pronounced in the 21st century.

So how have we maintained our own unique culture even through great influxes of immigrants in our history? The greater the influx of migrants, the more difficult it is to maintain a cohesive culture. This is simply a natural fact and important to note as the United States accepts a vastly greater number of immigrants than ever before. The greater the number of people from foreign soil, the greater number of differences in beliefs and philosophy will be present within any nation. But the solution to this dilemma is simple.

Our culture is founded in values, beliefs and a shared history in an ever-waged war against tyranny rather than simple bonds of race, ethnicity, or geography. Any free nation that long survives will ensure that its own people, along with those entering their borders, hold these same values and longing for liberty.

America gained the reputation of a melting pot not simply for diversity but also for assimilation. Migrants from across the globe brought their own gifts and strengths in art, music, food, work ethic, and commitment to God and family while striving to become Americans. Shared beliefs in religion, family values, morals, and ethics are absolutely essential to maintaining a culture. These beliefs need not be uniform, and alternative beliefs or values should not be completely discouraged. But if there is no agreement among the people on our foundational principles of how we ought to live our lives, there can be no unity, no peace, and no lasting nation.

In order for a unique and coherent culture to form, a people must also share a language. This means not simply speaking in the same tongue or dialect — although that is certainly helpful — but rather a shared understanding of what words mean. Over the past decade it has become commonplace to redefine words or shift their meanings and use to fit political goals. We have redefined institutions, words, and even basic scientific terms in order to advance agendas.

This realignment of words is not simply an annoyance or a distraction; it is a clear and present danger to a people who wish to live free. Those who control language control the conversation and the political debate. Those who control the debate cannot lose. Every dictator and tyrant throughout the deep and dark history of the world has understood this fact and has sought to redefine words to his own ends.

In the United States, as recently as this year, our own government has redefined the term "recession" to avoid the current economic condition from being labeled as such. In unison, large media outlets, paid economists, and even online dictionaries quietly changed their definition of the word to fall in line with the ruling regime. And it doesn't stop with economics. The term "vaccine" was redefined in 2021 by our own Centers for Disease Control and Prevention to conform to its latest efforts.

Long-standing institutions such as the Merriam-Webster dictionary have redefined even the most basic terms (such as "man" and "woman") in order to fall in line with radical factions within America and the western world. Any society that redefines such basic words in obvious political posturing will not long remain free, but will also not allow a people to live together with any lasting peace or understanding of one another.

So where is the source? Why do our shared culture, values and language continue to crumble, and our society collapse further into chaos? Because before anything else, a unified and free nation must hold a shared reality. A shared reality does not mean that every individual holds the same life experiences and economic or social status. Rather, it means that people view the world in front of them through a similar lens. Facts remain facts and what is natural and ordered is distinct and apparent.

In order to form bonds of brotherhood, maintain a cohesive society and form a foundation in which to confront and resolve our differences, we must share the same reality — also known as the truth. Once these basic building blocks of a nation are in place, they require constant maintenance as forces external and internal will try to destroy these pillars of society with one simple, tried and true weapon: division.

Any tyrant who has ever sought to conquer a nation or enslave a people has first thought to himself, "How can I weaken resistance?" There are many weapons of the tyrant. Disarm the opposition, spread lies, and instill fear. But no other method has ever produced the instant and long-lasting results as sowing division among the people. When Mao conquered China and Lenin oversaw the Bolshevik revolution, was their victory driven by soldiers and artillery or rather hatred and division? When these Communist dictators ruled over and enslaved the same people who fought for them, was it merely the fear of an iron fist that solidified their rule? Or rather an enduring flame of division and envy that was sown in their hearts?

The cunning dictator recognizes that while people will often do as they're told while looking down the barrel of a gun or the tip of a spear, they are only ever one moment away from realizing that they are many and their rulers are few. However, if people are kept at war with themselves — if he pits rich against poor, old against young, man against woman, educated against uneducated, race against race, religion against religion — they will never even realize that they are slaves. They will exhaust themselves in contrived battles and causes that offer an illusion of benefit or simply appeal to the human tendency to anger and resentment.

The endless list of human differences continues down an bottomless well, never running dry for the tyrants among us to dip into whenever they are in need. Often, these artificial divisions are based on some historical truth that the passions of man cannot leave behind in the dustbin of history. The tyrant not only sees the benefit of distraction and weakness but also a scapegoat to heap all of the common people's problems.

The tyrant will convince you that if your family is hungry, it is not because the government has failed to create a thriving economy; it is because someone who is wealthier than yourself has taken the food from your mouths. If your streets are not safe, it is not because the government has failed to adequately implement law and order; it is because individuals of other races don't want you in their safer neighborhoods. If you have not attained the education or social status you had hoped for, it is not because of government failures, personal choices, or uncontrollable life events; it is because a group more privileged than yourself is holding you down.

The list goes on and the well deepens. The tyrant wants you to believe that the real tyrant is your neighbor. He wants your finger pointed in every direction except his. The tyrant understands that even the oldest and strongest regimes are but a house of cards built on fear, lies, and division.

We are no strangers to division. We in America are pitted against one another daily based on race, religion, sex, lifestyle, income, social status, and every possible personal characteristic under the sun. Those who now control our government understand that they are at the doorstep of absolute authority. They understand that if this division continues to erode our bonds of brotherhood, they will never have to face legitimate opposition to their continued quest for dominion over us. But of all the forms of division we see today and of all that this world has ever seen, what is most powerful? The individual divided against himself.

It is a powerful thing to divide a population. To sow hate and instill rivalries that weaken opposition to a tyrant's rule. But when a tyrant sows division, his goal is not simply to create war and strife among the people. That is simply the result on the surface. The true goal is to create a raging war inside the minds and hearts of men. When man is divided within, he becomes hateful of himself. He becomes angry, aggressive, and volatile. He is quick to violence and slow to thought.

The purpose of division is to make man feel inadequate, insecure and not in control of his own life. In this quest for internal division, a tyrant confuses a man. The tyrant encourages the man to pursue destructive desires and habits that give birth to self-resentment. The tyrant tells a man to measure himself by his worldly comforts rather than his principles. The tyrant tells a man that reality itself is simply an illusion or social structure created to keep him in his place. These whispers continue on and on until man is so consumed by loathing, envy, and confusion that he lacks the vision or energy to fight his true enemy. If man is kept at war with himself within the confines of his own mind, the tyrant has already won.

A free nation will have its disagreements. It will have its battles on policy and rhetoric. But through war and peace, a free and just nation will stand firm against the cunning division of tyranny by holding true to eternal bonds of brotherhood and understanding.

Diagnosing Our Problems

Now, let us begin with the easiest of tasks: listing the problems before us. Volumes could be written simply evaluating the dangers now faced by America as we sink deeper into the pit. This list will be neither comprehensive nor meticulous in its diagnosis. It will, however, serve to evaluate our problems before we offer solutions. Let us proceed from fiscal to cultural.

The National Debt – Outside of a short period under Andrew Jackson, the United States has always operated with a certain amount of debt. However, today that debt stands at more than $31 trillion. Our yearly debt now towers over our GDP and some of our most powerful rival nations own a significant share of that debt. Despite generating record tax revenue year after year — exceeding $4 trillion in 2021 — we continue to run record deficits, as spending soared to nearly $7 trillion in

2021. Do you believe this money is being used appropriately, and do you think that any country can long survive this way?

Inflation – Cost of living in The United States rose by 7.1% in 2021 followed by another 6.5% in in 2022, the highest rate in more than 40 years. It was 7% in 2021. This means the average American family is losing roughly $5,000 per year of annual income as wage growth continues to stagnate and fall far short of inflation rates. Many economists now argue that using pre-1980s methodology, inflation rates are now exceeding 15% as the cost of gasoline has exploded by over 100%, crushing record highs, while grocery bills steadily climb. How much longer can the American family sustain this level of spending?

Wage Gap – The wealthiest 1% in America now owns a combined $45.9 trillion, nearly a full third of the nation's wealth. This number increased by more than $6.5 trillion in 2021 alone and $12 trillion over the course of the COVID pandemic and lockdowns. This happened while the bottom 90% of Americans lost wealth. Can a society function freely when so much power resides with so few, and can this type of wealth and power be attained without preferential treatment from the government?

Healthcare – The cost of our medical care continues to skyrocket more than any other industry in America, while patients face fewer options and often lower quality. The government and corporations now have more say over our medical decisions than ever before, and millions of people have been required to undergo medical procedures against their will. Does this sound like a patient-centered healthcare system?

Immigration – In 2021, more than two million illegal immigrants were encountered crossing our southern border. We then proceeded to smash all-time highs with three million in 2022. Estimates show 10 million to 12 million illegal immigrants now reside within our borders, making up 3% of the population. In addition, we are now accepting more than one million new legal immigrants to the United States every year. This mass immigration to America over the past several decades has represented the largest movement of people in human history.

On our southern border, an unchecked flow of crime, drugs, and human trafficking is joined at the hip with illegal immigration. The massive flow of foreign individuals has greatly dragged down wages and created cultural barriers, not only in language, but also in our way of life. Can any nation maintain a coherent culture and harmony with such a great and rapid influx?

Drug Addiction – More than 20 million American adults have at least one addiction. Since 1999, over one million Americans have died from overdoses. Drugs are now more accessible than at any time in our history, are glamourized in entertainment and media, and are increasingly being used among young children, as nearly half of U.S. minors use illegal drugs before they graduate from high school. In addition, children and adults are being prescribed psychiatric drugs and painkillers at alarming rates, smashing all-time records. Is this what a physically and mentally healthy society looks like?

Education – American education was once the envy of the world. Our scores and achievements in math, science, literature, and almost every field of study outpaced the rest of the globe. Today, America constantly ranks in the 20s and 30s among nations for math and science scores despite domestic spending on public education increasing by more than 150% since 1970. In some of our major cities, the majority of students are now illiterate, with areas such as Baltimore reporting that only 13% of 4th through 8th-graders are proficient in reading. In addition to our failing public school system, our higher education system is putting students into crippling debt without equipping them with adequate skills or matching them to lucrative jobs. Will our society remain prosperous without proper education?

Law and Order – The United States is in the grips of a violent crime wave, as 2021 saw more than 20,000 homicides — the highest rate in 25 years. Violent crime is up across the board, as aggravated assault has risen 12% in recent years, especially in our major cities, causing those with the means to flee to safer areas. This has come during a time when many major police departments have seen their budgets cut and heightened scrutiny of policing tactics has led to an officer shortage. If a government cannot provide basic safety for its people, how can it secure their rights?

Corruption – Our federal, state, and local governments — along with our political process — have become entirely corrupt. Massive corporations broker insider deals, enormous political action committees (PACs) sway elections, endorsements are bought and sold, and party leadership and committee assignments are doled out to the most prolific fundraisers.

Elected officials leave office to become highly paid lobbyists, insider trading is commonplace in Congress, and the vast majority of our government and legal system is controlled by unelected bureaucrats who have no accountability to the people. Does this sound like a government that will advocate for the welfare of the people?

Families – The family has, through all of human history, been the rock of society. For thousands of years we have known that a strong family is the key to a strong society. Today, the U.S. marriage rate is at an all-time low as more young adults are choosing polyamory or cohabitation without the commitment of marriage. Nearly a quarter of all American children are growing up in single-parent homes — 80% of them headed by single mothers. This is three times the global average and the highest rate in our history. Specifically in the African-American community, single motherhood has reached 70% or higher in many communities and, at large, the number of unmarried parents has quadrupled since 1968.

Across racial lines, the most accurate predictor of poverty and crime in a community or household is single-motherhood rates. Birthrates have fallen below replacement levels while we perform more than 600,000 abortions per year in America. Regardless of your opinion on the subject, having 600,000 or more unwanted pregnancies each year is an undeniable problem that must be addressed. When the family is devalued, will a nation long thrive?

The Public Square – We are supposedly living in the information age, but we are either drowning in excess or discovering only the information and opinions deemed appropriate by society's elites. Like it or not, big tech social media platforms have become the new public square, and while companies wish to present themselves as private corporations, they are, in fact, monopolies that operate as pseudo-government agencies.

We do not have the right to speak freely on social media platforms without the threat of censorship, suspension, or outright banning. Corporate media and social media platforms have dubbed the arbiters of their preferred information "fact checkers," who simply exist to defend the approved narrative. The opinions of the vast majority of Americans are now subject to censorship if they are uttered on big tech platforms, to corporate media, or in most any workplace. How can a society be free when a select few control the flow and validate the authenticity of information?

Our Elections – Today in America voters hold one of three beliefs about elections, depending on the election result and the voter's political party affiliation. The first is that our election system is safe and secure. The second is that fraud occurs, but to an unknown degree. The third is that our election system is totally and utterly rigged.

We often hear that more than 50% of Republicans believe the 2020 election was stolen from Donald Trump, but in addition, 42% of Democrats believe or once believed the 2016 election was stolen from Hillary Clinton. This tells us one thing with absolute certainty: Trust in our institutions and elections is at an all-time low. Can a people who distrust their own elections live peacefully with one another?

Our Basic Rights – As Americans, we have lost the right to control very fundamental aspects of our lives. We now live in a country where we can own our land but must pay taxes to reside on it. The government can heavily regulate or shut down our businesses on a whim and can ban worshipers from attending church for extended periods of time. Individuals (including children) can be forced to accept drugs against their will. The government attempts to form councils to regulate speech and infringes upon our right to self-defense. This is merely a snapshot of what has become an increasingly unfree society. Is this how self-government is supposed to operate?

Cultural Divide – The brokenness of our culture is the chief issue of our time. We can and we will use policy to address many of the problems facing America, but cultural problems are not solved through legislation alone. Today, we have individuals who hold the idea that men can be women and that children ought to be put on drugs to alter their hormones or have their genitals removed altogether. Teachers speak to 8-year-old children about sex and masturbation. Parents bring children to highly sexual drag shows and parades. Men dominate women in women's athletics. And as a direct or indirect result, we have a pedophilia wave that is undeniable.

Teachers also expose children to radical theories on race, leading them to resent themselves or others based on the arbitrary color of their skin and, increasingly, parents are told they do not have authority over their own children. Will a society that cannot agree on basic realities of life ever find peace?

Our problems are many and these are simply a few, but the picture it paints is that of a broken, immoral, and out-of-control government that seeks to not only empower and enrich itself, but also drain every ounce of authority away from the individual.

Repairing Our Government

The following three sections are inextricably linked, as our Republic cannot hope to be restored without drastic repairs within our halls of government, our culture, and our very souls. So let us work from the outside in. We have just discussed a portion of the problems facing our nation. This list alone would cripple the greatest of nations and thus far has weakened the United States more quickly than anyone could have imagined. Our status on the world stage is rapidly declining as we continue on this path to ruin.

What must be done to reform our government? The following is not a set of policy prescriptions, as countless manifestos have been written and re-written on those subjects. Instead, we must begin to think of what must change among the people.

We have spent our entire lives lamenting over the course of our nation. We complain that our institutions are crumbling and our representatives are corrupt and increasingly deaf to the needs and desires of the people. But in this lamentation, we fail to recognize that we all shoulder the blame. We have attempted to skirt responsibility by blaming big money and corrupt politicians instead of taking matters into our own hands. Do we not understand that every corrupt politician and every lifetime grifter has been elected and re-elected by us? The very people who increasingly feel disillusioned with their government are simultaneously empowering it.

Term limits perfectly illustrate this phenomenon in American politics. Public support for term limits may be the most unifying issue in America today, as 80% of voters are in favor, including the vast majority of both Republicans and Democrats. In all likelihood, those in Congress will never vote for term limits, as this would damage their own power and interests. We blame elected officials for failing to cure the rampant disease that is the lifetime politician. "Politics should not be a career," we rightfully claim.

Yet we are blind to the simple fact that we have the opportunity to "term limit" any politician we choose. We have the opportunity to vote out members of Congress in primary and general elections every two years. But when it comes time to enter that voting booth, the people will cast their ballots and the incumbent will emerge victorious in 95% of contests. We spend our lifetimes clamoring for fresh blood, new ideas, and accountability in Congress, but when push comes to shove, we have almost exclusively selected the 30-year incumbent over the fresh start we have been calling for.

Some will say, "The incumbents always win because they have the cash and connections." They would be correct. In recent history, the highest spenders in a Congressional race have won 95% of their races. Many will rightfully point to the much-needed reform in campaign finance, dark money, and super PACs. Without a doubt, elections are increasingly bought and sold, not won.

But why is money so effective? In addition to our claim to want fresh blood, we claim we want "outsiders," or candidates who aren't manipulated by big money. So why do we continue to elect the career politician who is manipulated by big money? The answer is that We The People have checked out of the political process. We are now less educated and engaged in political affairs than at any time in

American history.

Today, in our primary elections, it is not uncommon to have 10% to 15% voter turnout. In most primary races, the incumbent or highly funded candidate will have a challenger. Typically, this challenger will be minimally funded — an "outsider" — and have nearly no attachment to the corrupt political apparatus. In the minds of most people, this is the ideal candidate, but most voters will never hear of this challenger until they walk into the voting booth and proceed to fill in the bubble of the most recognizable name.

Why is this? Is it because we don't have access to information? We have a world of information at our fingertips 24 hours a day. We can intensely vet every candidate as we never could before. We can easily see where they are receiving and spending their money, we can see everything they've done in the past, and we can see every issue they claim to stand for.

Political clubs and organizations host numerous meet-and-greets for these candidates so voters can interact and ask questions directly. And today, every serious candidate has a website and social media accounts to learn and interact with. So, the question becomes, what is our excuse? Money, corruption, and endorsements are all easy targets on which to heap our displeasure.

Truly free people are not only engaged in their political process, but they are also critical and discerning thinkers. TV ads or fancy mailers will not easily sway an educated and engaged voting base. But today even the most educated and intellectual among us are easily fooled by fancy slogans, high-profile endorsements, and perceived prestige. That is because we have lost the ability to use our own thoughts and ideas, think critically, and come to conclusions. Like many areas of our modern life, we have grown accustomed to being spoon-fed. We rely on others, instead of our own faculties, to provide us information and ideas. The key to tyranny is turning off the minds of men. If you can convince the people that they are better off to doubt their lying eyes and rely not on their own intellect but rather trust those at the top who are considered wise and fair, you have already enslaved the people you wish to conquer. The greatest threat to an all-powerful government is a people who think for themselves. A mind becomes powerful when it becomes independent. A critical mind becomes whole when it is also discerning.

As we have seen time and time again, a crafty and shrewd politician will test the prevailing winds and use our own current emotions and ideals against us. He will say what needs to be said and play the part required to achieve his position, but when the time comes to act, he is nowhere to be found. These betrayals rarely come without warning signs. How often have we seen a politician spontaneously change his views or come around to a new way of thinking just in time to run for office? How many politicians, for example, will have made their entire fortune from China, only to campaign on being "tough on China?" These politicians are a dime a dozen, but we have failed to see through their thinly veiled charade.

Our two-party system has become more of a uniparty that holds one objective: to maximize and cement the power of the political establishment. Due to our lack of discernment, our political ruling class has become a country club. We are now represented almost exclusively by wealthy elitists who were elected simply because they were born into the right family, have the right connections, or have the proper number of zeroes in their bank account. In fact, that is all it takes to get the federal, state, and local party organizations on board. And since this will always be the case, the people are the final barrier to keeping these individuals and organizations in their place. But we have failed to do so. America is now trapped in a dystopian cycle where some puppets come and go, but the puppet masters remain.

This country club has become so firmly entrenched that it employs a full-time machine to ensure that any challengers remain on the outside. Unless anointed by the privileged few, a candidate is blackballed from donors, endorsements and media. The only answer — the only hope to save America from this stranglehold — is for the people to reject the demands of the ruling class, think for ourselves, and refuse to be fooled by the same song and dance that has been foisted upon the working class for decades. We The People have power, if we only choose to activate it.

Lastly, once we have engaged ourselves and rediscovered our ability to think critically and with discernment, we must raise the bar for our elected officials and demand better. Government is like any relationship in life — you will get what you tolerate. If you are in a relationship living with constant disrespect and abuse, and you fail to set clear standards or separate yourself entirely, you will continue to face the same disrespect and abuse on an ever-increasing scale. Man is a being that has a tendency to test his limits — to take an area of behavior as far as he can until he faces consequences. We see this in the smallest of children who, almost instinctively, test the patience and discipline of their parents. If a child misbehaves without consequence, he will continue one step further.

And whether in a relationship or child rearing, without standards or discipline, no course correction will be consensually undertaken. Can we not say this describes the current state of our government? Through our own apathy and our politicians' gaslighting, we have accepted the worst from our leaders. We have come to accept that corruption, incompetence and laziness are simply the status quo — as it always has been and always will be. While the worst among us with wicked intentions will always try to infiltrate the political arena, they have succeeded only because we have allowed them to.

The vision set out for America's leaders was the idea of the "public servant." We looked to government officials as our subordinates who were meant to generously give of themselves to represent the people for whom they cared. Indeed, at our founding, there was little to be gained from serving in our government other than personal pride and sense of purpose. It was not a path to immense wealth and fame. Those who took on the role of our representatives did so despite the negative impact it may have had on their financial prospects. This led us to elect individuals who had a greater interest in service than self.

But as government power and wealth grew, the temptation to throw off the yoke of public service became stronger. Today, the floodgates have opened while we have fallen asleep. We must restore this idea of "public service" and make our elected officials and those seeking office prove to us that they are motivated not by money and power but by an unwavering commitment to give of themselves. Let us begin to evaluate those who seek our vote not by their wealth, fame, or prestige, but by their work ethic, character, and commitment to service. Not just by their words, but by their actions.

If we return to these once-foundational principles, we will begin to see a government free of the charlatans, grifters and corruption that currently occupy our offices.

Repairing Our Culture

It is important to note that nothing stated in the previous section can hope to be accomplished without a great awakening within our culture. At our founding, Americans viewed government as a necessary evil — a structure that needed to be in place to secure our liberties but was best kept as far away from the home, church, and business as possible. It was once believed that the individual, families, and local communities were capable of caring, providing, and looking out for themselves, and that the federal government was mainly a hindrance to prosperity, happiness, and security.

This completely rational perception was borne out of the early Americans' own experience. In the early days of our republic, Americans had just endured many decades of harsh regulations that strangled their businesses, significant threats to free speech and press, and threats of armed force against self-government — all stemming from an all-powerful centralized government in which they had no representation.

For the first time, men could freely work, speak, worship, travel, and have control over their own lives. This not only sparked excitement and innovation, but led individuals to believe that life was not simply for surviving but thriving — that they were not at the mercy of arbitrary authorities, but beholden only to God, nature, and their own grit. This led men to take bold action — to venture west, to invent, to expand their enterprise, to educate their minds, and believe that they could leave this country better for posterity. For the very first time in human history, the power of the individual had been unleashed.

America launched into the future as no nation before it. Industry, invention, discovery, literature, art, and a spiritual renaissance boomed out of a once small colony. Just 150 years since its inception, the United States became the economic and military might of the world, all while preserving the greatest amount of freedom for its people.

But then something happened. Something changed. Seemingly overnight, we were no longer pioneers, no longer adventurers, no longer innovators or craftsmen. We became cogs in a great machine.

The government that was once viewed as a small but necessary irritant was embraced as a caretaker. We opened our homes, our businesses, and our houses of worship to the very government we fought to remove from our doorways. We began to believe not only that the government could improve our lives, but that we could not be prosperous or happy without it. Where we once valued individualism, opportunity, competition, adventure and virtue, we now valued conformity, security, safety nets, and fleeting pleasures.

We have increasingly been taught that we cannot get an education without government assistance, we cannot obtain property without government assistance, we cannot work or build a business without government assistance, we cannot raise a family without government assistance, we cannot retire without government assistance, and that we cannot make our own personal life decisions without government assistance. But the real tragedy is not that this way of thinking has been pushed on us — tyranny over the minds of men is an ever-existing and relentless force. The tragedy is that we now truly believe it. This belief has not only rendered us impotent in our own lives, but it also has empowered those few elites who, in their hearts, believe the opposite.

For the first time in American history, our people believe that we are at the mercy of the world. We believe that we are powerless to leave this country better than we found it, that we are unable to build a life worth living, and that we ought to simply squeeze as much temporary pleasure out of life as we can before we inevitably die and return to the earth. Simply, we are reverting to the natural state of humankind that would choose a false sense of security over the rigorous adventure of a life unleashed.

What is incredible, but too often understated about the foundations of American culture, is that our powerful sense of individualism was also once combined with an unwavering sense of responsibility to our families, communities, and fellow man. We once thought it our duty to look after our fellow man, to give him shelter when he needed warmth, food when he was hungry, and to lift him up when he was down. It was considered not only the action of a good man, but an obligation to raise up his neighbor. This was not simply looked at as a societal code or structure but rather a divine responsibility. We once believed we were placed on this earth specifically to help those around us, and we could not hope to fulfill our God-given purpose without putting others before ourselves.

This way of life offered (and still offers) not only an abundance of charity, but also an abundance of prosperity and peace. A sense of community and responsibility creates love and respect for one another that strengthens our bonds of brotherhood. It shows man that he is not alone in a world that can be cold and cruel; that when the winters of life come, his neighbor will welcome him to his fire. And not only among ourselves. When this sense of community exists among our citizens, it extends to our businesses and our government, keeping the human tendencies of greed and corruption at bay. Simply, we should seek to cultivate a society that values the individual and individuals who value their society.

Whatever sense of responsibility we once had must be rediscovered. We live in a time when the interests of "me and mine" reign supreme over all other beliefs and responsibilities. Today, people treat one another as threats or inconveniences to their personal security and pleasure. When we see poverty, we no longer seek to intervene for good, to look into our own hearts and pockets for what we may give. We look to an almighty and impersonal government to intervene on our behalf, for it is no longer our job to look out for others.

We, as Americans, have become solely motivated by material goods and physical pleasure. When evaluating our lives, we look to our bank accounts, our homes' square footage, our social media presence, our number of partners and everything above the surface. This is the view of modern success. No longer do we look to how much we give of ourselves, how many lives we have touched, how much love we give and how much our lives will matter after we have departed this earth. That is the measure of true success, and we used to know it.

As a result of our increasingly selfish society, we have been forced to live with increasingly crooked corporations and government. When people cease to care for one another, businesses seek only to maximize their bottom line. When people hold no respect for their neighbors, their government begins to view them as isolated animals.

Ultimately, we must end the culture in America that exists only to indulge selfish desires. Day by day we are seeing the consequences of a society that says, "Do whatever you want, sleep with whomever you want, indulge yourself however you want." How, at a time when we are purported to have more freedoms, comforts, and access to physical pleasure than ever before, are we experiencing record depression, anxiety, and loneliness? It is because we have forgotten what makes man truly happy, fulfilled and free. Sleeping with a stranger does not. Shooting up drugs does not. Undercutting a small business to marginally increase your bottom line does not. So, what does? Giving your all to someone you love does. Treating your body with respect does. Using your financial blessings to help others does. Harnessing your intellect and finding greater purpose does. We used to see these ideas for the truths that they are.

Our responsibility to one another and beyond ourselves is what made America great. A society that respects the lives and well-being of others will respect the rights and liberty of others. If you have no respect or sense of responsibility to your neighbor, will you fight for his rights? And when your other neighbor sees that you abandoned him, will he come to your aid? Society is indeed a chain that depends on our respect for one another to preserve our natural rights. Why do corrupt governments and usurpers attempt to sow division, hatred, and distrust amongst the people? To dissolve those bonds of respect and responsibility. Once the bond is broken and the institutions are taken, there is nothing to stop the impending assault.

Some will say, "How do my own personal decisions and actions affect this chain? As long as I am not hurting anyone else, I should be able to do what I please." I would answer, "Do you believe that you can respect others if you view them only as an assistance to physical pleasure, or will you begin to view them as objects or instruments? Do you believe that you can respect yourself when you are inhaling or injecting chemicals known to damage your body, brain, and behavior?"

Indeed, there is a policy debate to be had on what specific laws will be effective or helpful in practice, but without structure and expectation, without codes of morality or conduct, we will first lose our respect, followed by our rights, and conclude in a full collapse of any civilized and free nation as we have seen countless times throughout human history.

My statements in this section are not a revelation. They are not new or unique ideas. I do not claim to be a great arbiter of truth or justice. I am simply reaffirming what some would call foundational, basic or common sense. In order to maintain our republic and our God-given rights, we must restore a culture that values the independence of individuals and families, that looks to itself and its neighbors before the government, that thirsts for adventure and competition, that thinks critically, believes in the power and capability of the individual, that maintains a sense of community and responsibility to others and — most importantly — that respects the value and rights of its fellow man.

Most simply put: Love thy neighbor.

Repairing Our Spirit

We now enter into the very core, where humanity is created and destroyed. Where life and dreams spring, and fear and doubt are ever-awaiting. The soul of man is what will truly dictate the course of America. We can argue and bicker on tax policy and immigration, but until we have fixed ourselves, until we have healed our souls, all other solutions will simply be ineffective bandages.

Man is not a temporary being. We are not simply born, briefly animated, and buried. It is true that all men will die and that these bodies we are currently housed in are temporary and will someday return to the earth. But your life, no matter how you choose to view it, is eternal. Every thought, action, and decision you make in life will positively or negatively impact posterity. The way you choose to raise your child will live on for thousands of years. The impact of what you give and how much you love will ripple from lifetime to lifetime. The causes you fight for will shape the lives of millions born and unborn. And when your body goes to rest and someday your name is forgotten on this earth as all men before you, the spirit of your life will live on.

So why now do we regard our lives and our very souls so cheaply? Because, we have been taught by those who do not wish to see us prosperous and free that we are nothing more than cogs in a machine. That the wheels of life continue to turn and we are simply replaceable units that will be discarded into a bin when no longer useful. I am here to tell you, that is not who you are and that is not what you were created to be.

Each one of us was created with a unique and divine purpose. Have you ever stopped to think that you could have been born anywhere, at any time, at any place, to any family? The odds of you being born into your specific life are astronomical, but you were. Why? Is life just a random simulation with cells firing and burning out haphazardly until one day it just all ends without purpose? No. You were placed in this time, in this place, because you were given gifts, abilities and talents that no one else possesses. Repairing the soul of America begins with this great re-awakening — remembering that all of us are beautifully created with immeasurable potential and strength.

To begin this healing, we must first remember that we are all unique and powerful beings with a divine purpose. This can be very hard to see in our modern society, because from the time we are born, we are assigned a number and viewed by the government and corporations as more of a commodity than an individual. When we are young children, we are too often forced into daycare and raised by strangers without the necessary feelings of love and individual affection that humans require. As we go through school we are forced to learn and behave in a one-size-fits-all system that discourages individualism, creativity, and our unique skills.

After mandatory schooling, we are told that in order to be successful, we must take on massive debt and select a course of study and field of work for the rest of our lives at the age of 18. We then go to work, where we travel on packed roadways into dense cities, funnel into massive high-rise widget factories, cram ourselves into tiny cubicles, stare emptily at screens for 9+ hours and drive home just so we can do it again the next day. And when we finally get home, we flip on our TVs and scroll through our phones, immersing ourselves in the state-approved culture and narratives, putting the final nail in the coffin of our dreams, ideas, and unique abilities.

All of this takes place while corporations generate record profits, the government rakes in record taxes, and the family takes home less and less. Once you take a step back from this way of life, you begin to realize that you are viewed more as livestock than man. Some may say this is the end state of capitalism, but can any system be called capitalist that is ruled by massive monopolies that seek to squash small businesses, inventors, and individual entrepreneurship? This is the end state of an oligopoly.

As if peering into our future, Alexis de Tocqueville wrote in 1835, *"After having thus successively taken each member of the community in its powerful grasp, and fashioned them at will, the supreme power then extends its arm over the whole community. It covers the surface of society with a net-work of small complicated rules, minute and uniform, through which the most original minds and the most energetic characters cannot penetrate, to rise above the crowd. The will of man is not shattered, but softened, bent, and guided: men are seldom forced by it to act, but they are constantly restrained from acting: such a power does not destroy, but it prevents existence; it does not tyrannize, but it compresses, enervates, extinguishes, and stupefies a people, till each nation is reduced to be nothing better than a flock of timid and industrious animals, of which the government is the shepherd."*

We didn't get here because of a deep state. We didn't get here because the elites are more gifted or intelligent. We got here because, somewhere along the line, we decided it would be easier to shut off our brains and hop on the hamster wheel. We decided that as long as we have a roof over our heads, food in our belly and something to watch on a screen, we would not seek any more from life. That is the default state of mankind, but not the default state of Americans.

We once knew that we are powerful. We knew that individuals and families are capable of accomplishing great things. That within our very souls are mighty gifts that we only need discover and put to use. We once knew that we are unique, that our lives and gifts are irreplaceable, and that no government, business, or human being could ever match us. And above all, we once knew that we are born with a divine purpose.

What is a divine purpose? We have many purposes in our lives day to day. We eat, we sleep, we work — all to fulfill a basic purpose or need that is naturally occurring in life. But a purpose that is divine is a purpose much greater than ourselves. When we live out a God-given purpose, it creates waves of positive impact to ourselves and others. Taking on a divine purpose means taking on a great responsibility, but with an even greater reward. When you lie in your bed at night and imagine yourself creating riches to elevate your family and charity to others — that is a divine purpose. When you fight for a cause that will make others free, prosperous and happy — that is a divine purpose. When you sacrifice and give of yourself to leave a legacy behind for your grandchildren's grandchildren — that is a divine purpose.

Your divine purpose is something that lives inside you and only you, that requires your own unique skills, ability, and grit to bring to life and that leaves yourself, your family, and this world better than you found it. We each carry this purpose, a mission handed down to us — but only we can make it a reality. This is the core of American greatness. Independence, Manifest Destiny, the ideas of unleashing power and ability in one great purpose making a lasting impact. That is not only what Americans once believed; it is what we lived for. And we must live for it again.

Once purpose is restored, this great machine that has crippled our minds and stifled our abilities will begin to lose its control. But in order to live out this purpose we must first find courage. Courage is the prerequisite to all other virtue. You cannot stand up for what you believe without courage to face those who oppose you. You cannot build a business without having the courage to face failure. You cannot raise a family without having the courage to provide and protect. You cannot even love if you do not first find the courage to make yourself vulnerable.

Nothing worth doing in our lifetime will be done without courage. This does not mean being free from doubt or fear. Rather it means taking action in the face of your doubts and fears. Most cultural issues in America today can be boiled down to a lack of courage. In the same way a father abandons his child because he lacks the courage to uphold his responsibility, we, as a whole, have lacked the courage to stand in the face of tyranny and oppression.

We recently lived through a time when it was commonplace and acceptable for the United States government to close a private business without any consent or legislation. As a result, hundreds of thousands of small businesses were permanently destroyed and millions of Americans were plunged into poverty. Many would rightly argue that the government's actions were unconstitutional and violated private property rights, yet it acted without significant opposition. Business owners grumbled and complained, but less than 1% took action. If these owners, employees, and communities had found the courage to refuse to shut down and to operate their private businesses in a way they deemed fit, the government would have been powerless to stop them.

But when a people live without courage — when we live in our fears and value our material comforts over our basic liberties — the government can do what it pleases, when it pleases. The only buffer to government overreach is the courage of the people. At times, we forget the only reason we are here today is due to the courage of those who came before us. The courage of the men who signed our Declaration of Independence, the courage of the soldiers who fought to end slavery, the courage of women and blacks who demanded equality under the law, and the courage of our ancestors who ventured the seas to escape tyranny.

Our politicians are the living and breathing example of a life without courage. The rulers in our local, state, and federal governments are nearly all completely beholden to their parties, mega-donors, and lobbyists. They are terrified of losing their seat at the table and have abandoned any sense of courage to do what is right for the people they have pledged to serve. We, as an American people, must have the courage to stand on our own two feet and proudly proclaim the rights and responsibilities that are inherently our own. No longer can we bow in the face of injustice, the ruling elite, or the hostile mob. If we truly believe in liberty, we must live life with unwavering courage.

Once we have finally rediscovered our power, purpose, and courage, we must embrace the final piece — virtue. When you look to any great society, you will first see a strong, independent, driven, and virtuous people. Truly good people inherently create good government and respectable businesses. Conversely, when a nation is comprised of a people solely motivated by their own selfish desires, you will see only corruption, poverty, violence and sorrow.

We can look to the depravity and decadence of ancient Greece and Rome. We can look to the unquenchable thirst for riches, power and authority of the British and French empires. And we can now turn to our own backyard as our once-great American cities burn and collapse under the weight of their own debauchery. This collapse of the American nation is not simply taking place because the wrong people are in charge. For our entire past, present and future, there will be individuals with evil intent attempting to grab the levers of power and steer society to fit their own desires.

What has happened is that we have allowed these same individuals to wield our own selfish and base desires against us. One who is slave to his desires will also be slave to his government. That is why moderation, temperance and ultimately virtue are essential to a free society. When a man is consumed by his desires, his greed, his lust, he is unable to discern the consequences of his actions until they are beyond his control. When a man is slave to lust, he will abandon his rights and responsibilities in order to satisfy himself, no matter how temporary. When a man is slave to indulgence, he will harm others and himself in his quest for gratification.

But when a man knows virtue, he will suppress his own selfish desires that lead only to brokenness. A virtuous man knows that temporary pleasure is not freedom or fulfillment. In fact, it is often the opposite. When we craft a life that is concerned only with satisfying our physical selves, we create our own cage. This cage comes in many forms. It comes in our own lives as we cannot advance ourselves beyond these desires. It comes as a barrier to healthy relationships with others, and it eventually becomes a tool of a tyrannical government to keep us dependent upon its supply for our addictions.

Every man serves someone and worships something. The only choice we have is what that will be. Will we choose to succumb to our base desires and regard ourselves as nothing more than animals to be pacified? Or will we view ourselves as higher beings who are endowed with power, potential, and purpose and whose adherence to virtue creates prosperity for ourselves and those we love?

Remembering Who We Are

"I am well aware of the toil and blood and treasure, that it will cost Us to maintain this Declaration, and support and defend these States. Yet through all the Gloom I can see the Rays of ravishing Light and Glory. I can see that the End is more than worth all the Means. And that Posterity will tryumph in that Days Transaction, even altho We should rue it, I trust in God We shall not."

As John Adams wrote these words and sent them from Philadelphia to his wife in Boston, the signers of our Declaration stirred in their beds with fear and anticipation for what the sunrise would bring. It was July 3, 1776: the final day of an unfree America.

Place yourself in this moment. These men — some of the greatest minds in human history — gathered together to make a choice. A simple choice, but by no means an easy one. They understood that when they arose the following morning, they might just as well be walking themselves to the gallows. Each and every man gathered in Independence Hall understood the gravity of what he was about to undertake. They understood that they were attempting to defeat and cast out the most powerful military force the world had ever seen. They understood that as soon as they put their pen to our Declaration, a death sentence was now upon themselves and their families.

But beyond anything else, they understood that they were not claiming something new or abstract. They were not seizing or capturing. They were simply asserting what ought to be. It was not simply that man could be free — it was that we ought to be free. That liberty is the natural right of man despite the words of any parliament or king.

The intellect, discernment, selflessness, strength, purpose, courage and virtue displayed by these men is what laid the groundwork for the greatest, most free and prosperous society this world has ever seen. I submit to you that the same principle resides in us — that this virtue flows within our very blood and soul as Americans.

We are the people who threw off the yoke of

tyranny and oppression, armed with little more than patriotism and courage. We are the people who fought and died so that the stain of slavery might be lifted from our land. We are the people who crammed into carts and wagons to venture into the unknown, to seek out adventure and abundance. We are the people who sailed oceans so that our children could know what it means to be free.

We are the people who bled on far away beaches so that the free world would not fall. We are the people who took to the streets to ensure equality under the law so every man, woman, and child could live the life God intended. We are the people who put men on the moon and led the world in invention and innovation never seen before. We are the people who have never seen an obstacle too large or challenge too difficult to overcome.

We have greatness in our very bones.

Now is the time to remember.